Learn Japanese with Stories
Volume 5:
Shitakiri Suzume

plus

Kobutori Jiisan

Clay & Yumi Boutwell

Copyright © 2010-2021 Kotoba Books

www.TheJapanShop.com

www.MakotoPlus.com

ISBN: 1490938974

ISBN-13: 978-1490938974

INTRODUCTION

The key to learning vocabulary is, quite simply, reading. Not only are you more likely to pick up words that interest you, but you also learn them in context. The Japanese Reader Collection was designed for this purpose.

FOR BEGINNERS

This reader is for upper beginner students of Japanese. Beginners can get a lot out of it, but we recommend learning hiragana first. We are also including furigana (small kana over kanji) and romaji so you can be sure you are reading with the correct pronunciation.

MP3s

Included, at no extra charge, are MP3s of the story. One is read at the normal speed and the other at a slow, easy to follow speed. If the MP3s were not included when you purchased this book, please see the last page for a download link. If you have ANY trouble downloading, please email us at help@thejapanshop.com.

ABOUT THIS BOOK

Shitakiri Suzume follows a common theme in Japanese fairy tales: a childless old couple raising a son or daughter. But instead of a human, the story revolves around a sparrow, the loving pet of the old man. Also common with other tales, there is a moral to the story. Don't be greedy!

This book contains several versions of the story. First, we have the story with every vocabulary word defined and explained. Next, we go through major grammatical patterns found in the story. After that, read the story with no English and in natural Japanese (kanji with furigana included). Lastly, we are including a simple English translation, which should be avoided until you are sure you understand the story or if you find it too difficult to figure out on your own.

You may want to try to read the story in natural Japanese first. Or if you are a beginner, it may be better to go through the vocabulary first. Any way you do it, this book offers several ways to read, listen, and learn.

Lastly, we would love to hear from you. If you have any suggestions to make this and other books better, please let us know.

Clay & Yumi Boutwell

help@thejapanshop.com

http://www.TheJapanShop.com

http://www.TheJapanesePage.com

https://www.MakotoPlus.com

CONTENTS

舌切り 雀

したき　　すずめ

Story Read Slowly

Story Read Normal
Speed

Scan the QR codes for instant and
FREE access to audio recordings

The Cut-Tongue Sparrow with Definitions

舌切り雀
<small>したきり すずめ</small>

むかし、むかし、あるところにおじいさんとおばあさんがいました。

―――

むかし、むかし a long time ago [a very typical opening for Japanese fairy tales similar to "Once upon a time"]

あるところに in a certain place

おじいさん an old man [invariably there is an おじいさん and an おばあさん in these stories! Remember use いる for living things and use ある for non-animate objects]

と and

おばあさん an old woman

が [grammar marker—usually marks the subject]

いました there was; there existed

おじいさんは、とてもこころの優^{やさ}し

い人^{ひと}でしたが、おばあさんは

たいそういじわるな人^{ひと}でした。

―――

おじいさん an old man

とても very

こころの優しい人 a very nice person [tender-hearted person; as in English, こころ, heart, is used as the base of emotions; by contrast, the おばあさん is an いじわるな人]

でした past of the copula, です

が but; however [the が here is the conjunction meaning "but." It is used to show a strong difference between two things. The particle が comes right after the word or phrase it modifies; the conjunction が comes at the end of a complete thought/phrase.]

おばあさん an old woman

たいそう very

いじわる mean; bullying

人 person

おじいさんは、1羽の雀を大切に飼っていました。毎日毎日、まるで自分の子供のように世話をしていました。

おじいさん an old man

1羽 one bird (羽 is the counter for birds) [Birds are counted using 羽 wa, most animals use 匹 hiki (piki, biki after certain numbers)]

雀 sparrow [一羽の雀 (one sparrow)]

大切に carefully

飼っていました owned (a pet) [Owning/taking care of a pet uses the verb 飼う kau. Don't confuse this with the verb to buy 買う kau.]

毎日、毎日 every day; day after day [the word is repeated for emphasis]

まるで it is just as if; just like [this is a very useful construction: まるで別人でした。 marude betsujin deshita. It was as if he was a different person; ように [youni—like; similar to] is often found with まるで]

自分の子供 one's own child

のように just like

世話をしていました took care of

ある日、おじいさんが出かけて
いる間、おばあさんは洗濯をして
いました。

———

ある日 one day
出かけている間 while out [*aida*—while...; during...]
おばあさん the old woman
洗濯 washing clothes
していました was doing

洗濯に使おうと用意していた のりを、おじいさんの雀が、すっかり全部なめてしまったので、おばあさんはたいへん怒りました。

———

洗濯 washing clothes

に使おう used for the purpose of (washing)

用意していた prepared (the starch)

のり starch

を [grammar: sets the direct object (Obaasan was preparing the starch)]

おじいさんの雀 the old man's bird

すっかり totally

全部 all; every bit [paired with *sukkari* for emphasis]

なめてしまった licked it up [なめる *nameru*—to lick; the しまった indicates completeness (and regret): licked it all up]

ので therefore; because of that

おばあさん old woman

たいへん very

怒りました became angry

おばあさんは、雀を捕まえて「この舌がそんな悪いことをしたんだね。切ってしまおう。」

―――

雀 sparrow

捕まえて caught

この舌 this tongue

そんな悪いこと such a bad thing

悪いことをしたんだね did a bad thing, didn't you? [the んだ is a shortened form of のだ and is used when giving explanations]

切ってしまおう I'm going to cut it off [the おう ending shows intent of the speaker]

といって、むりやり舌を切ってしまいました。

雀は、「いたい、いたい」と泣きながら、どこかへ飛んでいってしまいました。

といって saying that…

むりやり by force

切ってしまいました cut it all off [the *shimaimashita* shows both completion and regret]

雀 sparrow

いたい it hurts

と quotation marker

泣きながら while crying [ながら *nagara* (while) is added to the –*masu* form of verbs (minus the –*masu*) – 泣きます [*nakimasu* cry] -> 泣き + ながら]

どこかへ to somewhere [adding the か shows uncertainty: いつか *itsuka* someday; だれか *dareka* someone]

飛んでいって flew off

しまいました [an auxiliary verb after the ~*te* form that shows completion as in, "it completely flew off"]

帰ってきたおじいさんは、雀を探しましたが、家にはいません。

「おばあさん、雀はどこへいったかな？」と聞くと、おばあさんは、昼間のことを話しました。

帰ってきた returning back

探しました searched for

が but

家にはいません isn't at home

どこへいったかな？ where do you think (the bird) could have gone?

と聞くと asking A leads to B [the first と marks the quotation; the second expresses the meaning of, "And what followed was…"]

昼間 afternoon

昼間のこと about what happened in the afternoon [こと *koto* is used to mean "the situation" or "the circumstances"]

話しました told (the story)

「私の大事なのりをすっかりなめてしまったものだから、舌を切っておいだしましたよ。」

私の my

大事 important

私の大事なのり my important starch

すっかり completely

なめてしまった licked [*nameru* (to lick) + *shimau* (a verb that shows completion or regret.)]

もの [もの or もん (usually children's speech) is used when explaining and stressing something as being important]

だから therefore; because of that

舌 tongue

切って cut

おいだしました drove away [追い出す]

舌を切っておいだしましたよ (I) cut the tongue and drove the bird away [切って *kitte* (cut and then) 追い出しました *oi dashimashita* (drove away)]

おじいさんは、「それはかわいそ
うなことをした。雀は、大丈夫か
な。」と、大変がっかりしました。

それは (as for) that

かわいそう pitiful; too bad [often かわいそうに *kawaisou ni* is used by itself to mean, "That's terrible" or "I feel so bad for…"]

かわいそうなことをした (You) did a pitiful thing [The こと makes かわいそうな a noun phrase and therefore, something that can be done.]

雀 sparrow

大丈夫かな (I) wonder if (the bird) is all right

大変 very

がっかりしました disappointed [a very similar word (perhaps a different form of the same word) is がっくり which means basically the same thing—disappointment; hopes dashed…]

おじいさんは、雀のことが心配でたまらず、探しにでかけました。

雀のこと about the sparrow

心配で with worry

たまらず can't stop [dying for…, itching for…; examples: 心配でたまらず worried sick; the ず ending is another way to make the negative; add たまらない after the ~たい form of a verb: 旅行したい I want to travel. -> 旅行したくてたまらない I'm just dying to travel.]

雀のことが心配でたまらず can't stop worrying about the sparrow

探しに to go look for [The *ni* shows purpose: for the purpose of searching]

でかけました left; departed

探しにでかけました left to search for

山の中を歩きながら、「舌切り雀の

お宿はどこだ、ちゅんちゅんちゅ

ん。」と探し回りました。

山の中 in the mountains

歩きながら while walking

舌切り雀 cut-tongue sparrow

お宿 residence [polite form; add お before nouns (usually 訓読み

kun'yomi—native Japanese words); many such words have become

words in their own right: お酒 osake; お茶 ocha]

〜はどこだ where is …?

ちゅんちゅんちゅん chirping sounds

と quotation marker

探し回りました going around searching [many verbs are combined

with other verbs in Japanese to expand the meaning; he wasn't just

searching, but he was searching around; 探す sagasu (search) + 回る

mawaru (go around)]

ずいぶん長い間、そうやって探していると、どこからか、

「舌切り雀のお宿は、ここだ。ちゅんちゅんちゅん。」と聞こえてきました。

ずいぶん fairly; pretty (long time)

長い間 a long time

そうやって in that way

探していると upon searching

どこからか out of somewhere

ここだ is here

と quotation marker

聞こえてきました was able to hear

おじいさんが、その声のするほうに行ってみると、そこにはかわいらしい雀のおうちがありました。

———

その声 that voice

のする what is doing (the voice)

ほうに in the direction of (the voice)

行ってみると upon going to see… [〜みる means "try doing" or "to do"]

そこに at that spot; there

かわいらしい cute; lovely

雀 sparrow

おうち house (polite)

ありました there was [polite past of ある *aru*—to exist]

家の前ではあの舌を切られた雀が
おじいさんを待っていました。

家の前で in the front of the house

あの that

舌を切られた雀 the sparrow whose tongue was cut [*kirareta* is the passive construction of 切る *kiru*—to cut]

おじいさんを待っていました was waiting for the old man [The を sets the old man as the direct object, the reason for the sparrow's waiting.]

「おじいさん、ようこそいらっしゃいました。」

「おお、お前^{まえ}が心配^{しんぱい}で、ずっと探^{さが}していたんだよ。」

おじいさん the old man

ようこそいらっしゃいました welcome [the sparrow always speaks very politely]

おお oh

お前 you

心配で to be worried about

ずっと for a long time

探していたん looked [The *n* ender is used when explaining something—often with emotion.]

だ [the plain past form of the copula *desu*]

よ [ender showing emphasis]

「それはそれは、ありがとうご

ざいます。さ、こちらへお入<ruby>入<rt>はい</rt></ruby>りくだ

さい。」

それはそれは as for all that [doubled for emphasis]

ありがとうございます thank you

さ well, then

こちらへ this way

お入りください please come in [polite form; お + *masu* form of verb

without *masu* + ください]

雀に案内されて、家の中へ入ったおじいさんは、雀の兄弟や家族、友達から大歓迎をうけました。

雀に by the sparrow

案内 guide

雀に案内されて was guided by the sparrow

家の中へ入った (the old man who) entered the house

雀の the sparrow's [The *no* shows relationship between the two nouns.]

兄弟 brothers (and sisters)

や and

家族 family

友達 friends

兄弟や家族、友達から from the brothers, family, and friends

大歓迎 a big welcome

うけました received (a big welcome)

おいしいお料理^{りょうり}に、とても楽^{たの}しい雀^{すずめ}の踊^{おど}り。おじいさんは、大喜^{おおよろこ}びで過^すごしていましたが、「もう日^ひも暮^くれる。

———

おいしい delicious

お料理 food (polite)

とても very

楽しい fun

雀の踊り sparrow's dance

大喜びで with great fun

過ごしていました spent (time)

が but

もう日も暮れる already the sun is setting [もう *mou* (already); 日も *hi mo* (the sun also…); the old man is giving a reason but using も may mean he has other reasons in mind too.]

そろそろ帰る<ruby>帰<rt>かえ</rt></ruby>ることにしよう。」と言<ruby>言<rt>い</rt></ruby>いました。

———

そろそろ soon [often said by itself to show a desire to leave]
帰ること leaving; the act of leaving
にしよう let's decide on (leaving) [にする is used when making decisions]
帰ることにしよう I'm leaving.
と言いました said

雀たちは、「せっかく来てくださったのですから、今夜はここにお泊まりください。」と引き止めました。

雀たち sparrows (plural)

せっかく with great trouble; especially; with kindness [せっかく is a word that isn't easily translated. It is often used as in this case to show appreciation for the effort or value of something someone did. "You went through all the trouble of getting here, so (please stay)."]

せっかく来てくださったのですから since you came out of your way to visit here

今夜 tonight

ここに here

お泊まりください please stay (polite)

と引き止めました said while trying to stop him (from leaving) [the most common use of the question marker と is perhaps と言います [to iimasu—to say], but Japanese allows for any number of ways to color the meaning of "He said,"]

でも、おじいさんは、「いやいや、おばあさんも待っていることだし、今日は帰ります。また、遊びにきますよ。」

でも but

いやいや no, no

待っている waiting

こと [turns *matteiru* (to wait) into a noun phrase: waiting]

だし and [the plain form of *desu* with *shi* which is used for listing reasons or excuses]

今日は as for today

帰ります to leave

また again

遊びに for the purpose of playing (visiting) [the common way to say, "to visit" from 遊ぶ *asobu* (play); the に shows intent or purpose]

きます to come; will come

よ [ender showing emphasis]

「そうですか、それは残念です。では、おみやげをお持ちいたしましょう。」

　雀は、奥からつづらを二つ出してきて、おじいさんに尋ねました。

———

そうですか is that so

それは as for that

残念です too bad; regretful

おみやげ souvenir; parting gift

お持ちいたしましょう take with you

雀 sparrow

奥から from the back

つづら basket; trunk [a つづら could be a basket, trunk, or to make it sound better for the gist of the story—a chest]

二つ two (trunks)

出してきて brought out

おじいさんに to the old man

尋ねました asked

「こちらに重^{おも}いつづらと、軽^{かる}いつづらがあります。どちらがよろしいですか？」

こちらに here we have…

重いつづら a heavy trunk

と and

軽いつづら a light trunk

があります there are; there exists

どちら which

どちらがよろしいですか？ Which would you like? [polite; same as どっちがいいですか？ *docchi ga ii desu ka?* Which is better?]

おじいさんは、「私は、もう年だし、帰りのみちのりも遠い。軽いつづらにしよう。」

こう言って、おじいさんは、軽いつづらをもって帰りました。

おじいさんは as for the old man

私 I

もう年だ I'm already old [another common expression is いい年 meaning a "good old age": もういい年のでやめてください。 *mou ii toshi node yamete kudasai*. You're getting on up there, so please stop (doing something dangerous).]

し and [used when giving a series of reasons or excuses]

帰りの道のり the journey home

も also

遠い far

軽いつづら the light trunk

〜にしよう (I) choose; to decide upon

こう言って saying that, he…

もって帰りました carried (trunk) and went home

おばあさんは、おじいさんの帰(かえ)りが遅(おそ)いので、「いったいどこへいったのだろう。」とぶつぶついいながら待(ま)っていました。

おばあさん the old woman
おじいさんの the old man's
帰りが遅い being late in returning
ので therefore
いったい just what is…? [いったい *ittai* is another tricky word to flatly translate. It is used to give emphasis to the sentence. In cases like this, "ever" is a good working word. Where EVER did he go, I wonder? It is best to learn words like this by examples: いったいどうしてそんなことを言った *ittai doushite sonna koto o itta?* Why ever did you say such a thing? いったいだれがしたのか？ *Ittai dare ga shita no ka?* Whoever did that?]
どこへいった where did he go?
だろう I wonder…
いったいどこへいったのだろう I wonder just where did he go?
ぶつぶつ murmuring
いいながら while saying…
待っていました was waiting

そこへ、おじいさんがおみやげのつづらをもって帰ってきました。

「おじいさん、いったいどこへ行っていたのですか？」

そこへ there (at that moment)

おみやげ souvenir; gift

つづら trunk

もって帰ってきました came back home carrying...

いったい just; where/what in the world?!

どこへ to where

行っていた went

いったいどこへ行っていたのですか？ Just where have you been all this time?!

「今日は、雀のお宿へ行って、おいしい料理や雀の踊りを見てきたよ。それにこんなおみやげまでもらったよ。」

今日は today

雀の the sparrow's

お宿 residence (polite)

へ行って went to…

おいしい料理 delicious food

や and

雀の踊り sparrow's dance

見てきた went and saw

よ [ender showing emphasis]

それに in addition to that

こんな this; such (a wonderful gift)

それにこんなおみやげまで on top of all that, they even gave me such a wonderful gift [the こんな and まで expresses the thought of "to such an extent"]

もらった received

おばあさんは、つづらをみると、急 に機嫌がよくなって、「おや、まあ、そうでしたか？いったい何が入っているんでしょうね。」と、いいながら、つづらのふたをあけました。

つづらをみると Upon seeing the trunk…

急に suddenly

機嫌がよくなって became a good mood [機嫌 *kigen* (mood) can be good or bad: 機嫌が悪い *kigen ga warui* (Bad mood) or 機嫌がいい *kigen ga ii* (To be in a good mood)]

おや、まあ well, now

そうでしたか is that so?

いったい just; what in the world?! [the old woman suddenly starts speaking politely; notice the use of いったい in a positive, inquisitive sense.]

何 what

いったいなにがはいっているんでしょうね I wonder what ever could be in it.

いいながら while saying

ふた lid

あけました opened

すると、中にはたくさんの金や銀、さんごといった宝物が入っていました。

―――

すると upon doing so… [すると *suru to* is one of those nice action phrases. Doing that… happened. Another oft heard phrase in story telling is そのとき *sono toki*—Just then…]

中に inside

たくさん much; many

金 gold

や and; such things as…

銀 silver

さんご coral (used as a decoration)

といった such as… [といった *to itta* such as, like… [と言った] similar to という but with a stronger emphasis]

宝物 treasure

入っていました was inside

おじいさんもおばあさんもびっくりしてしまいました。

おじいさんは、「いや、驚いた。

も also

びっくり surprised

いや wow [showing surprise]

驚いた was surprised

帰りに、雀がつづらを二つ出してきて、「重いほうと軽いほうとどちらがいいですか？」と聞くから、わたしは軽いほうを選んだんだよ。」と、おばあさんに話しました。

―――――

帰りに when leaving

二つ出してきて brought out two

重いほう the heavy one

軽いほう the light one

どちらがいい which is better

と聞くから because (the sparrow) asked

わたし I

選んだ chose

おばあさんに話しました (He) said to the old woman

おばあさんは、その話を聞く

と、怒って言いました。「どうして

重いほうをもらってこなかったんで

すか？もっとたくさんの宝物が入

っていたにちがいないじゃありませ

んか。」

その話 that story

聞くと upon hearing

怒って angrily

言いました said

どうして why

もらってこなかった didn't come back with

もっと more

たくさん many

宝物 treasure

たくさんの宝物 more treasure

入っていた would be inside (the trunk)

にちがいない without doubt

じゃありませんか isn't it?

次の日、おばあさんは、雀の宿へ出かけていきました。「舌切り雀のお宿は、どこだ？ちゅんちゅんちゅん」。

———

次の日 the next day

雀の the sparrow's

宿へ toward the house

出かけていきました left; departed

舌切り雀 the cut-tongue sparrow

どこだ？ where is

ちゅんちゅんちゅん chirping sounds

すると、「舌切り雀のお宿は、ここだ。ちゅんちゅんちゅん」と聞こえてきました。おばあさんが声のするほうに行ってみると、舌を切られた雀が家の前で待っていました。

———

すると upon doing so

お宿 house; residence

ここだ here

ちゅんちゅんちゅん chirping sounds

と聞こえてきました began to hear (chirping)

声 voice

ほうに in the direction of

声のするほうに in the direction of the voice

行ってみると went to see and...

舌 tongue

切られた was cut (passive)

家の前で at the front of the house

待っていました waiting

「おばあさん、ようこそいらっしゃいました。どうぞお入りください。」

おばあさんが中へ入ると、雀たちがお料理や踊りの用意をしています。

ようこそいらっしゃいました welcome [even after all the old woman has done, the sparrow is still very polite]

どうぞ please; this way

お入りください please come in

中へ toward inside

入ると upon entering [The と means "the old woman enters and then … happened."]

雀たち the sparrows

お料理 cooking

や and; things like this

踊り dancing

用意 preparations (for dancing and food)

しています were doing

でも、おばあさんは、「そんなものは、どうでもいい。早くおみやげのつづらをだしておくれ。」と雀をせかしました。

でも but

そんなもの such things

どうでもいい never mind that; inconsequential; all that's trivial

早く quickly

おみやげ souvenir; gift

つづら trunk

だしておくれ bring them out!

と quotation marker

せかしました to rush; hurry up

雀は、しかたなくつづらをふたつ出してきて、「そうですか、それでは、重いほうと軽いほう、どちらがよろしいですか？」と聞きました。

———

しかたなく without a choice

つづら trunk

ふたつ two

出してきて brought out

そうですか is that so?

それでは well, then

重いほう the heavy one

と and [choose between the two choices; or]

軽いほう the light one

どちら which

よろしい good; fine [which do you choose?]

と聞きました asked

おばあさんは、「それはもちろん

重(おも)いほうだ。」と、さっそくそれを

背中(せなか)に担(かつ)いで出(で)て行(い)ってしまいまし

た。

———

それは as for that

もちろん of course [もちろん [*mochiron*—of course] is used to show
the old woman thinks the other choice (light chest) would be foolish]

さっそく immediately; at once

それ that

背中 (one's) back

担いで carry; to shoulder

出て行って left out

しまいました shows completion (she left completely)

おばあさんは、重いつづらを背
負って歩いているうちに、ずいぶん
疲れてしまいました。

——

重い heavy

つづら trunk

背負って carry on one's back; to be burdened

歩いている walking

うちに while; during

ずいぶん fairly; pretty

疲れてしまいました was completely tired

山道の途中で、「これは、とっても重い。いったいどのくらい宝物が入っているか、見てやろう。」と、座ってつづらのふたを開けました。

———

山道 a mountain road

の途中で while on the way (on the mountain road)

これは as for this

とっても very [an emphasized version of とても]

いったい just...; what in the world?

どのくらい about how much

宝物 treasure

入っている entered; inside (the trunk)

か an ender adding uncertainty (wonder what's inside)

見てやろう let's have a look

と座って said and sat

つづら trunk

ふた lid

開けました opened

すると、中<ruby>なか</ruby>から気味<ruby>きみ</ruby>の悪<ruby>わる</ruby>いおばけが
たくさん飛び出<ruby>とだ</ruby>してきて、「この
欲張<ruby>よくば</ruby>りばばあめ。」と、おばあさん
を脅<ruby>おど</ruby>かしました。

———

すると upon doing so

中から from the inside

気味の悪い disgusting [like 機嫌, 気味 uses の悪い to complete the thought. 気味の悪い can mean weird, creepy, grotesque, etc.]

おばけ ghosts; spirits; monsters

たくさん many

飛び出してきて began to jump out

この this [referring to the old woman]

欲張り greedy [欲 *yoku* (desire; greed) + 張り *hari* (stretch, grow); another similarly constructed word is: 頑張る *gan baru* 頑 *gan* (harden; strengthen) + 張る *baru* (stretch, grow)]

ばばあ old hag [a more casual and rude form of おばあさん]

め [a derogatory suffix; 〜め *me*—a rude suffix to belittle someone: こいつめ *koitsume*—that jerk; ばかめ *bakame*—idiot]

脅かしました threatened; surprised

おばあさんは、「ひやー、たすけてくれー。」と叫びながら、山道を走って逃げていきました。

おしまい。

ひやー yikes (sound of screaming)

たすけてくれー please help

と叫びながら while shouting [~*nagara* adds "while" to the meaning]

山道 a mountain road

走って ran

逃げていきました ran away

おしまい the end

The Cut-Tongue Sparrow *in Japanese*

舌切り 雀
<small>したき　すずめ</small>

　むかし、むかし、あるところにおじいさんとおばあさんがいました。おじいさんは、とてもこころの優しい人でしたが、おばあさんはたいそういじわるな人でした。

　おじいさんは、１羽の雀を大切に飼っていました。毎日毎日、まるで自分の子供のように世話をしていました。

ある日、おじいさんが出かけている間、おばあさんは洗濯をしていました。洗濯に使おうと用意していたのりを、おじいさんの雀が、すっかり全部なめてしまったので、おばあさんはたいへん怒りました。おばあさんは、雀を捕まえて「この舌がそんな悪いことをしたんだね。切ってしまおう。」といって、むりやり舌を切ってしまいました。

雀は、「いたい、いたい」と泣きながら、どこかへ飛んでいってしまいました。

　帰ってきたおじいさんは、雀を探しましたが、家にはいません。「おばあさん、雀はどこへいったかな？」と聞くと、おばあさんは、昼間のことを話しました。「わたしの大事なのりをすっかりなめてしまったものだから、舌を切っておいだしましたよ。」

　おじいさんは、「それはかわいそうなことをした。雀は、だいじょうぶかな。」と、大変がっかりしました。

　おじいさんは、雀のことが心配でたまらず、探しにでかけました。

山の中を歩きながら、「舌切り雀のお宿はどこだ、ちゅんちゅんちゅん。」と探し回りました。ずいぶん長い間、そうやって探していると、どこからか、

「舌切り雀のお宿は、ここだ。ちゅんちゅんちゅん。」と聞こえてきました。おじいさんが、その声のするほうに行ってみると、そこにはかわいらしい雀のおうちがありました。家の前ではあの舌を切られた雀がおじいさんを待っていました。

「おじいさん、ようこそいらっしゃいました。」

「おお、お前が心配で、ずっと探していたんだよ。」

「それはそれは、ありがとうございます。さ、こちらへお入りください。」

雀に案内されて、家の中へ入ったおじいさんは、雀の兄弟や家族、友達から大歓迎をうけました。おいしいお料理に、とても楽しい雀の踊り。おじいさんは、大喜びで過ごしていましたが、「もう日も暮れる。そろそろ帰ることにしよう。」と言いました。

雀たちは、「せっかく来てくださったのですから、今夜はここにお泊まりください。」と引き止めました。でも、おじいさんは、「いやいや、おばあさんも待っていることだし、今日は帰ります。また、遊びにきますよ。」

「そうですか、それは残念です。では、おみやげをお持ちいたしましょう。」

雀は、奥からつづらを二つ出してきて、おじいさんにたずねました。

「こちらに重いつづらと、軽いつづらがあります。どちらがよろしいですか？」

おじいさんは、「私は、もう年だし、帰りのみちのりも遠い。軽いつづらにしよう。」

こう言って、おじいさんは、軽いつづらをもって帰りました。

おばあさんは、おじいさんの帰りが遅いので、「いったいどこへいったのだろう。」とぶつぶついいながら待っていました。そこへ、おじい

さんがおみやげのつづらをもって帰ってきました。

「おじいさん、いったいどこへ行っていたのですか？」

「今日は、雀のお宿へ行って、おいしい料理や雀の踊りを見てきたよ。それにこんなおみやげまでもらったよ。」

おばあさんは、つづらをみると、急に機嫌がよくなって、「おや、まあ、そうでしたか？いったい何が入っているんでしょうね。」と、いいながら、つづらのふたをあけました。

　すると、中にはたくさんの金や銀、さんごといった宝物が入っていました。おじいさんもおばあさんもびっくりしてしまいました。おじいさんは、「いや、驚いた。帰りに、雀がつづらを二つ出してきて、「重いほうと軽いほうとどちらがいいですか？」と聞くから、わたしは軽いほうを選んだんだよ。」と、おばあさんに話しました。

　おばあさんは、その話を聞くと、怒って言いました。「どうして重いほうをもらってこなかったんですか？もっとたくさんの宝物がはいっ

ていたにちがいないじゃありません
か。」

　次の日、おばあさんは、雀の宿
へ出かけていきました。「舌切り雀
のお宿は、どこだ？ちゅんちゅんち
ゅん」。すると、「舌切り雀のお宿は、
ここだ。ちゅんちゅんちゅん」と聞
こえてきました。おばあさんが声の
するほうに行ってみると、舌を切ら
れた雀が家の前で待っていました。

　「おばあさん、ようこそいらっし
ゃいました。どうぞお入りくださ
い。」

　おばあさんが中へ入ると、雀たちがお料理や踊りの用意をしています。でも、おばあさんは、「そんなものは、どうでもいい。早くおみやげのつづらをだしておくれ。」と雀をせかしました。雀は、しかたなくつづらをふたつ出してきて、「そうですか、それでは、重いほうと軽いほう、どちらがよろしいですか？」と聞きました。

　おばあさんは、「それはもちろん重いほうだ。」と、さっそくそれを背中に担いで出て行ってしまいました。

　おばあさんは、重いつづらを背負って歩いているうちに、ずいぶん疲れてしまいました。山道の途中で、「これは、とっても重い。いったいどのくらい宝物が入っているか、見てやろう。」と、座ってつづらのふたを開けました。すると、中から気味の悪いおばけがたくさん飛び出してきて、「この欲張りばばあめ。」と、おばあさんを脅かしました。

　おばあさんは、「ひやー、たすけてくれー。」と叫びながら、山道を走って逃げていきました。

　おしまい。

The Cut-Tongue Sparrow *English Translation*

<ruby>舌<rt>した</rt>切<rt>き</rt>り 雀<rt>すずめ</rt></ruby>

Please try to tackle the Japanese first and use this only as needed.

A long time ago, in a certain place, there lived an old man and old woman. The old man was kind-hearted, but the old woman was fairly mean.

The old man tenderly kept a sparrow as a pet. Every day, he took care of it as if it were his own child.

One day, while the old man was out, the old woman was washing clothes. Because the sparrow had eaten up all the starch, the old woman was very angry. The old woman caught the sparrow and said, "This tongue did such a bad thing. I will cut it off!"

While crying, "It hurts! it hurts!", the sparrow flew away somewhere.

The old man came back looking for the sparrow but didn't find him at the house.

"Old woman, I wonder where the sparrow went?" he asked her. She told him about what happened that afternoon.

"He ate my important starch and so I cut his tongue."

The old man said, "That is such a pitiful thing you did. I wonder if the sparrow is all right." He was very disappointed.

The old man couldn't stop worrying about the sparrow and set off to look for it. While walking in the mountains, he searched and said, "Where is the Cut-Tongue Sparrow's house? Chirp, chirp, chirp."

After a long while of searching like that, from somewhere, he heard, "The Cut-Tongue Sparrows house is here. Chirp, chirp, chirp."

The old man went in the direction of that voice and there was a cute sparrow's house. In front of the house, the Cut-Tongue Sparrow was waiting for the old man.

"Old man, welcome!"

"Oh, I've been so worried, I searched everywhere for you."

"Well, I thank you for that. Please, come inside."

Being led by the sparrow, the old man entered and was welcomed by the sparrow's brothers, family, and friends. There was delicious food and an enjoyable sparrow dance. The old man greatly enjoyed the time, but he said, "The sun is setting. I must go soon."

The sparrows said, "Since you took so much trouble to come here, please stay the night."

But the old man said, "No, no. The old woman is waiting and all. I will go back today. I will come back again."

"Is that so? That's too bad. Well then, let's give you a souvenir."

The sparrow brought two trunks from the back and asked the old man.

"Here is a heavy trunk and a light one. Which do you choose?"

The old man said, "I'm old and the trip back home is long. I'll choose the light one."

Saying that the old man picked up the light trunk and went home.

Noticing the old man was late in returning, the old woman grumbled, "I wonder just where he went to?" Just then, the old man came home with the souvenir trunk.

"Old man, just where have you been off to?"

"Today, I went to the sparrow's house and had delicious food and saw dancing. In addition, I got this souvenir."

The old woman, upon seeing the trunk, suddenly adjusted her attitude. "Well, now. Is that so? I wonder what ever could be inside it," she said while opening the trunk's lid.

Inside was gold, silver, precious coral, and other treasures. The old man and old woman were surprised. The old man said, "Wow, I'm surprised. When leaving, the sparrow brought out two trunks. 'Would you like the heavy or the light trunk?' they asked. I chose the light one."

The old woman upon hearing the story said angrily, "Why didn't you bring back the heavy one? Surely it had even more treasure."

The next day, the old woman took off for the sparrow's house. "Where is the Cut-Tongue Sparrow's house? Chirp, chirp, chirp."

And then, she heard, "The Cut-Tongue Sparrow's house is here. Chirp, chirp, chip."

The old woman went in the direction of the voice and there was the sparrow whose tongue had been cut waiting for her.

"Old woman, welcome. Please come in."

The old woman entered, and the sparrows began to prepare food and dancing when the old woman said, "I don't need all that. Hurry up and bring out the presents."

The sparrows, not having a choice, brought out two trunks. "Which would you like? The heavy one or the light one?"

The old woman said, "Of course, the heavy one!" and quickly carried the trunk out the door. While carrying the heavy trunk on her back, she became very tired. While on the mountain road, she said, "This is very heavy. I wonder just what kind of treasure is in it! I'll take a look." She sat down and opened it.

Upon doing so, many disgusting evil spirits flew out from the trunk. "You greedy old hag!" they said threatening her.

The old woman screamed, "Hiya!! Help me!" and ran away.

The end.

Kobutori Jiisan with Definitions

こぶとりじいさん

Story Read Slowly

Story Read Normal
Speed

Scan the QR codes for instant and FREE access to audio recordings

むかし、むかし、あるところに、たいへんほがらかで、気のいいおじいさんが住んでいました。

——

むかし、むかし a long time ago [the repetition makes this a very long time ago]

あるところに in a certain place [a common beginning for fairy tales]

たいへん very

ほがらか cheerful

で and [he was both cheerful and had a good spirit]

気のいい a nice disposition

おじいさん old man

住んでいました lived

おじいさんは、たのしい 話 をし
たり、踊りを踊ったりするのがとて
も好きで、いつもにこにこしていま
した。

———

たのしい fun; interesting

話 a story

〜をしたり doing things like... [~*tari* is used when listing examples, but not a complete listing]

踊りを踊ったり things like dancing

とても very

好き like

で and [the で connects the fact that he likes dancing and talking with the fact he always smiles]

いつも always

にこにこ smile

ところが、このおじいさんにはひとつ悩<small>なや</small>みがありました。

———

ところが but; however [ところが means "however" or "nevertheless" and is made up of ところ (place; situation) and が (the conjunction "but")]

このおじいさんには for (regarding) this old man [には – these are two particles working together. The に shows who or what is receiving the action (the old man) and the は sets the topic (also the old man).]

ひとつ one

悩み problem; worry

ひとつ悩みがありました (he) had one worry

それは、おじいさんのほっぺに大<ruby>大<rt>おお</rt></ruby>き
なこぶがあったのです。

それは that was...

ほっぺたに on his cheek

大きな a big...

こぶ lump; bump

のです (explanation) [The ~*no desu* is used to explain what it was
that worried the old man. It often shows emotion. This problem was
important to the old man.]

普段はあまり気になりませんが、仕事をして疲れてくると、こぶが重くて肩がこってきます。

普段 usually; normally

あまり not very much (ends with a negative verb)

気になりません don't mind; don't pay attention to

が but; however

仕事 work

つかれて tired...

くると become… and...

仕事をしてつかれてくると when (he) gets tired from his work…

重くて heavy...

肩 shoulder

こってきます become stiff [the て indicates supposition: if this, then this; the きます means "to become"]

重くて肩がこってきます heavy shoulders become stiff (neck)

「だれかこのこぶをとってくれん

かのー。」おじいさんは、いつもひ

とりでつぶやいていました。

———

「」 quotation markers

だれか someone

このこぶ this lump

とってくれんかのー won't (someone) take this (lump) away? [This is the old man's dialect for 取ってくれませんか (won't you please take this). くれる is a common verb when asking favors. It means "to be given; to do for one". Here, it is in the polite negative since he is asking a favor.]

ひとりで by himself; all alone

つぶやいていました was grumbling

ある日、おじいさんがいつものように森で木を切っていると、急に雨が降ってきました。

——

ある日 one day

いつものように like always; in the usual way [ように ~you ni requires a の after nouns; other examples: あなたのように anata no you ni— like you; 冬になったように fuyu ni natta you ni—it is as if it became winter]

森で in the forest

木を切っていると cutting a tree and…

急に suddenly; all of a sudden

雨がふってきました it started to rain

「ひやー、これはひどい雨<ruby>雨<rt>あめ</rt></ruby>だ。たまらんのー。」

　おじいさんは、あまやどりをするために大<ruby>大<rt>おお</rt></ruby>きな木<ruby>木<rt>き</rt></ruby>のほらにはいりました。

―――

ひやー ah!

これは this is...

ひどい雨 a terrible rain

たまらんのー can't bear; unendurable (たまらない)

あまやどり shelter from rain

あまやどりをするために in order to take shelter from the rain

大きな木 a big tree

ほらに hole (in a tree); a hollow; a cavity

はいりました entered

「どれ、雨（あめ）がやむまでここで一休み（ひとやす）しよう。」

―――

どれ well; okay [*dore* as is used here really doesn't have a meaning other than to give the man a moment to reflect. (Let me see... Well, now... Hmmm...) But the word itself means "which (of three or more choices)"]

雨がやむまで until the rain lets up

ここで here; at this spot

一休みしよう (I'll) rest; take a break

おじいさんは、日ごろの疲れが出たのか、そのうちに眠ってしまいました。

―――

日ごろ everyday…; usual…; daily

疲れ tiredness; fatigue

日ごろの疲れ the usual fatigue [の is a powerful particle that indicates a possessive and creates a noun phrase of related nouns. Even if it isn't natural in English, sometimes thinking of の as 's (apostrophe S) can help. "The day's fatigue" or "being tired from a day's work."]

出た came out (the fatigue)

のか (explains why he fell asleep—because he was tired)

そのうちに eventually

眠ってしまいました feel completely asleep

雨がやんで、日も暮れて、お月様
がでても眠っていました。どれくら
い時間がたったでしょうか。

———

雨がやんで (even when) the rain stopped

日も暮れて (even when) the sun set

お月様がでても even when the moon came out

眠っていました (he was still) sleeping

どれくらい how much (how long)

時間 time

たったでしょうか (how much time) had past? [The でしょうか
deshou ka shows uncertainty and asks a rhetorical question, "who
knows how long?"]

なにやら、あたりが騒がしくなっ

てきました。ぴーひゃら、ぴーひゃ

らと笛の音も聞こえてきます。

　おじいさんは、その音でふと目を

覚ましました。

なにやら something（なにか）

あたり around; the vicinity

騒がしくなってきました began to make sound; become noisy

ぴーひゃらぴーひゃら sound of a flute

と the "quotation" marker for the sound

笛 flute; a pipe

音 sound

も also

聞こえてきます began to hear… [*kikoeru* means to be able to hear; to be heard; to be audible. The *kimasu* adds "began to…". You can think of it as "to come" or "become."]

その音で by that sound; because of that sound

ふと suddenly

目を覚ましました woke up

「ありゃー、いかん、どれくらいねむっていたのかな。」と、目をこすりながらあたりをみまわすと、それはそれはおどろきました。

———

ありゃー oh! (show of surprise)

いかん this is no good

どれくらい how much; how long

ねむっていたのかな (I) wonder how long I slept.

と quotation marker (shows where the quote ends)

目をこすりながら while rubbing his eyes

あたり around; the vicinity

みまわすと and looking around...

それはそれは that's… (stresses the fact he was surprised)

おどろきました was surprised

木のほらの周りでは、たくさんの鬼たちが集まって酒盛りをしていたのです。

木のほら the hole in the tree

周りで around (the tree)

たくさん many

鬼たち the onis; the ogres

集まって gathered

酒盛り drinking and partying; merrymaking

のです (used with explanations)

おじいさんは、みつからないよう
に、ほらの中（なか）で息（いき）をひそめてじっと
していましたが、

―――

みつからないように in order to not be found [This is the negative
form of みつかる *mitsukaru*—to be found; to be discovered. ように
you ni—in order to (meet a goal); so that...]
ほらのなかで inside the hole
息をひそめて hold (his) breath
じっと fixedly; firmly; steadfastly
が but; however

鬼たちの楽しそうに踊っている様子をみているうちに、自分もついつい踊りだしたくなりました。

鬼たち the onis; the ogres

楽しそうに in a fun way; looks enjoyable [adding そう *sou* to the –*masu* form of verbs and the adjective stem adds the meaning of "seeming" or "having the appearance of..."]

踊っている dancing

様子 way; state; circumstance

みているうちに while watching...

自分も he, himself also [we are seeing things from the old man's perspective so 自分 *jibun* refers to himself. He also...]

ついつい inadvertently; heedlessly; without thought [ついつい *tsuitsui*—unconsciously; by mistake; against one's better judgment; unintentionally]

踊りだしたくなりました began to want to dance

とうとう我慢(がまん)できなくなったおじいさんは、鬼(おに)たちの間(あいだ)に出(で)ていって、踊(おど)りだしてしまいました。

———

とうとう at last; finally

我慢できなくなった lost self-control; couldn't suppress (his desire to dance) [我慢 *gaman* is an important word in the Japanese mind. It means "patience" or "endurance"]

鬼たちの間に in the midst of the onis

でていって came out

踊りだしてしまいました came out dancing (shows slight regret) [The だした *dashite* comes from だす *dasu* meaning "to go out" and adds a sense of jumping or going out. He went out and danced. The しまいました *shimaimashita* shows completion of an action, but often—as in this case—it shows regret.]

「おや、こんなところに人間のじ
いさんがいるぞ。」

「よーし、食ってしまえ。」

———

おや oh? (show of surprise)

こんなところに in such a place as this

人間 human

じいさん old man [Normally, you should use *ojiisan* since we want to
be polite when referring to older men]

ぞ adds force (sentence ender; masculine)

よーし ok! (the ー is added to emphasize)

食ってしまえ eat up (male speech)

「いや、待て待て、なかなかおも
しろい踊りじゃ。しばらく見ていよ
う。」

―――

いや no

待て待て wait; hold up!

なかなか fairly; very

おもしろい fun; interesting

踊りじゃ dancing

しばらく a while

見ていよう let's watch

鬼たちは、おじいさんの踊りがお
もしろいので、げらげら笑いながら
ずっと見ていました。

——

おじいさんの踊り the old man's dancing

おもしろい fun; enjoyable

ので therefore

げらげら笑い laugh uproariously

ながら while

ずっと for a long time

見ていました were watching

「おもしろいじいさんじゃ、それ、

みんなで踊ろう。」

鬼たちもおじいさんと一緒になっ

て踊りだしました。

———

おもしろいじいさんじゃ Isn't he an interesting old man?

それ there!; look!

みんなで everyone together

踊ろう let's dance!

鬼たちも the onis also

と一緒になって came all together (onis and the old man)

踊りだしました came out and danced

時がたつのも忘れ、鬼たちとおじいさんは踊っていましたが、そのうちどこかでにわとりがなきました。

——

時がたつ time flies by; the passing of time

の that (makes the preceding into a noun phrase)

も even (forgot the time)

忘れ forgot

時がたつのも忘れ they even forgot the time

そのうち soon; before long

どこかで from somewhere

にわとり chicken

なきました crowed

「そろそろ夜が明ける。今日はもうおしまいにしよう。」

そろそろ soon; in a short time

夜が明ける dawn breaks

今日は today

もう now; already

おしまいにしよう let's call it a day

「いや〜。じいさんのおかげで今日は楽しかった。明日もぜひ来いよ。」

___

いや〜 oh!; my!

じいさんのおかげで thanks to the old man

今日は楽しかった today was fun

明日も tomorrow also

ぜひ by all means

来いよ come

おじいさんは、鬼がこわかったの
で、「へへー、明日も来ます。」と
返事をしました。

_____

鬼がこわかった (he) was scared of the onis [This is an example of the
が *ga* not marking the subject of the sentence, but the object. が *ga*
marks something important, and, in this case, that is the object of the
sentence.]

ので therefore

へへー eh

明日も tomorrow also

来ます (I will) come

と question marker

返事 answer

鬼のひとりが「いや、もしこないといけないから、なにか預かっておこう。そうだ、そのほっぺのこぶを預かろう。」

———

鬼のひとり one of the oni

いや well...

もしこないと if you don't come

いけない is no good

から therefore

なにか something

預かっておこう let's keep something; take something on deposit

そうだ I know!

その that

ほっぺのこぶ the lump on your cheek

預かろう let's take for safekeeping

そういっておじいさんのほっぺ
のこぶをとってしまいました。

　「いいか、明日来たら返してや
るぞ。」

――

そういって saying that...

とってしまいました took it away

いいか you hear?; got it?

明日きたら when tomorrow comes

返してやるぞ I'll give it back to you

おじいさんは、かるくなったほっぺをなでながら、大喜びで家に帰りました。そして、この話をとなりのおじいさんにしました。

かるくなった became light

ほっぺ cheek

なでながら while rubbing (his cheek)

大喜びで with great joy

家に to home

帰りました returned

そして and then

この話 this story

となりのおじいさんは、「いいこ
とをきいた。わしも鬼にこのこぶを
とってもらおう。」

　というのも、このおじいさんにも
ほっぺに大きいなこぶがあったので
す。

___

となりのおじいさん the old man next door

いいことをきいた I heard a good thing; that sounds good

わしも me too

鬼に to the onis

このこぶ this lump

とってもらおう have them take it

というのも because

このおじいさんにも this old man too

ほっぺに on his cheek

おおきな a big

こぶ lump

となりのおじいさんは、話に聞いたとおりの場所に行って、木のほらに座って、ずっと鬼が来るのを待っていました。

———

話 talk; speech

聞いた heard

とおり just like

場所 place

話に聞いたとおりの場所 the exact spot heard in the talk

に行って (he) went to

木のほらに in the hole of the tree

すわって sat

ずっと a long time

鬼がくるの the coming of the onis

待っていました waited

そして、夜、鬼たちがやってきて、酒盛りを始めると、鬼たちの間に出て行って踊りを踊り始めました。

———

そして and then

夜 evening

やってきて finally came

酒盛り feastmaking; drinking and partying

始めると started and…

鬼たちの間に in the midst of the onis

出て行って came out

踊りを踊り始めました started to dance

ところが、その踊りのへたなこと。

そのおじいさんは、陰気で意地悪で、人前で踊りなんて踊ったことがなかったのです。

ところが but; however

その踊り that dance

へたなこと was an unskilled thing; not good at (dancing)

そのおじいさん that old man

陰気で not cheerful; melancholy [this で connects the descriptors (conjunction: and)]

意地悪で ill-natured [this で is also a conjunction]

人前で in front of people [this で shows the location (in front of people)]

踊り dance

なんて such as!

踊ったことがなかった hadn't danced (before people) before

鬼たちは、「へたくそな踊りだな。なんだ、ちっともおもしろくない。それ、これを返すからさっさと家にかえれ！」

———

へたくそ poor at; awful

なんだ what's all this?

ちっとも at all; not... at all

おもしろくない not interesting

それ well then

これ this

返すから give it back to you so...

さっさと quickly; hastily; speedily

家にかえれ！ get home!

そういって、きのう預かったこぶをなげつけました。

すると、そのこぶはおじいさんのもう片方のほっぺにぺたりとくっついてしました。

———

そういって saying that...

きのう yesterday

預かったこぶ the lump we kept

なげつけました threw and stuck (to cheek)

すると and then...

もう片方 the other side

ぺたりと slap (the lump on cheek)

くっついてしました stuck; attached

おじいさんは、「こぶがふたつに
なってしまったよ。」と泣きながら、
家に帰っていったということです。

おしまい。

ふたつになってしまったよ became two (lumps)

と quotation marker

泣きながら while crying

家に to (his) house

帰っていった went home

ということです and that is that

おしまい the end

Kobutori Jiisan *in Japanese*

こぶとりじいさん

　むかし、むかし、あるところに、たいへんほがらかで、気のいいおじいさんが住んでいました。

　おじいさんは、たのしい話をしたり、踊りを踊ったりするのがとても好きで、いつもにこにこしていました。

　ところが、このおじいさんにはひとつ悩みがありました。それは、お

じいさんのほっぺに大きなこぶがあったのです。

普段はあまり気になりませんが、仕事をして疲れてくると、こぶが重くて肩がこってきます。

「だれかこのこぶをとってくれんかのー。」おじいさんは、いつもひとりでつぶやいていました。

ある日、おじいさんがいつものように森で木を切っていると、急に雨が降ってきました。

「ひやー、これはひどい雨だ。たまらんのー。」

おじいさんは、あまやどりをする
ために大きな木のほらにはいりまし
た。

「どれ、雨がやむまでここで一休
みしよう。」

おじいさんは、日ごろの疲れが出
たのか、そのうちに眠ってしまいま
した。

雨がやんで、日も暮れて、お月様
がでても眠っていました。どれくら
い時間がたったでしょうか。

なにやら、あたりが騒がしくなっ
てきました。ぴーひゃら、ぴーひゃ

らと笛の音も聞こえてきます。

おじいさんは、その音でふと目を覚ましました。

「ありゃー、いかん、どれくらいねむっていたのかな。」と、目をこすりながらあたりをみまわすと、それはそれはおどろきました。

木のほらの周りでは、たくさんの鬼たちが集まって酒盛りをしていたのです。

おじいさんは、みつからないように、ほらの中で息をひそめてじっとしていましたが、鬼たちの楽しそう

に踊っている様子をみているうちに、

　自分もついつい踊りだしたくなりました。

　とうとう我慢できなくなったおじいさんは、鬼たちの間に出ていって、踊りだしてしまいました。

　「おや、こんなところに人間のじいさんがいるぞ。」

　「よーし、食ってしまえ。」

　「いや、待て待て、なかなかおもしろい踊りじゃ。しばらく見ていよう。」

　鬼たちは、おじいさんの踊りがお

もしろいので、げらげら笑いながら
ずっと見ていました。

　「おもしろいじいさんじゃ、それ、
みんなで踊ろう。」

　鬼たちもおじいさんと一緒になっ
て踊りだしました。

　時がたつのも忘れ、鬼たちとおじ
いさんは踊っていましたが、そのう
ちどこかでにわとりがなきました。

　「そろそろ夜が明ける。今日はも
うおしまいにしよう。」

　「いや～。じいさんのおかげで今
日は楽しかった。明日もぜひ来い

よ。」

　おじいさんは、鬼がこわかったので、

　「へへー、明日も来ます。」と返事をしました。

　鬼のひとりが「いや、もしこないといけないから、なにか預かっておこう。そうだ、そのほっぺのこぶを預かろう。」

　そういっておじいさんのほっぺのこぶをとってしまいました。

　「いいか、明日来たら返してやるぞ。」

おじいさんは、かるくなったほっ
ぺをなでながら、大喜びで家に帰り
ました。そして、この話をとなりの
おじいさんにしました。

となりのおじいさんは、「いいこ
とをきいた。わしも鬼にこのこぶを
とってもらおう。」

というのも、このおじいさんにも
ほっぺに大きいなこぶがあったので
す。

となりのおじいさんは、話に聞い
たとおりの場所に行って、木のほら
に座って、ずっと鬼が来るのを待っ

ていました。

　そして、夜、鬼たちがやってきて、酒盛りを始めると、鬼たちの間に出て行って踊りを踊り始めました。

　ところが、その踊りのへたなこと。

　そのおじいさんは、陰気で意地悪で、人前で踊りなんて踊ったことがなかったのです。

　鬼たちは、「へたくそな踊りだな。なんだ、ちっともおもしろくない。それ、これを返すからさっさと家にかえれ！」

　そういって、きのう預かったこぶ

をなげつけました。

　すると、そのこぶはおじいさんの
もう片方のほっぺにぺたりとくっつ
いてしました。

　おじいさんは、

　「こぶがふたつになってしまった
よ。」と泣きながら、家に帰ってい
ったということです。

　おしまい。

Kobutori Jiisan *in English*

こぶとりじいさん

A long time ago in a certain place, there lived a very cheerful and good-spirited old man. The old man loved to tell interesting stories and dance. He was always smiling.

However, this old man had one problem. That was, on his cheek was a huge lump. Usually, he didn't mind it so much, but when he was tired from work, his lump became heavy and his shoulders became stiff.

"I wonder if someone could take this lump away from me," the old man would always say to himself.

One day, the old man was in the forest cutting trees as normal when suddenly, it started raining.

"Yikes! This is a bad rain. Too much!"

The old man took shelter from the rain in a hollow cavity in a big tree. "Well, I'll just take a rest here until the rain stops."

The old man was tired from the day's work and soon fell asleep. The rain stopped, the sun set, the moon came out and he still slept for however long it was.

Something in the area began to make noise. Pi-pyara... Pi-pyara—he heard the sound of a flute. The old man woke to that sound.

"Oh! This is no good. I wonder how long I slept." He rubbed his eyes as he looked around. What he saw surprised him. All around the hollow tree, there were many onis gathered drinking and partying.

The old man held his breath and stood still in the tree as to not be discovered. But, the onis were having so much fun dancing, he began to want to dance too. Eventually, he couldn't take it anymore and leapt out to the onis and began dancing.

"Oya... There's a human old man here."

"Yeah. Let's eat him."

"Wait. His dance is interesting. Let's wait and watch a bit."

The onis enjoyed the old man's dance and just laughed while watching him. "He's a funny old man. Let's all dance!"

The onis and the old man started dancing together.

Time slipped by as the onis and the old man danced. At some point, a rooster crew. "It is almost morning. I should call it quits today."

"Naw. Because of you, we had a lot of fun. You must come back tomorrow."

The old man was scared of the onis and said, "Um... I'll... come tomorrow."

One of the oni said, "Well, just in case you don't come back, we should take something from you as ransom. I'll take that lump on your cheek." Saying that, the oni took the lump from his cheek.

"You understand? If you come back tomorrow, I'll give it back."

While rubbing his light cheek, the old man went back home with great joy. He told his story to the old man next door.

The old man next door said, "I learned a good thing. I'll also go to the oni and get my lump taken away." This old man also had a large lump on his cheek.

The old man next door went to the place he had heard about and sat in the cavity of the tree, waiting for the oni to come.

And then, at night, the onis came, drinking and partying. The old man jumped out dancing. However, his dancing was very bad.

That old man was not very cheerful and didn't dance in front of people.

The onis said, "What a horrid dance. Not interesting in the least. Hey, we'll give this back to you. Go home!"

Saying that, they threw the lump they had taken the day before at him. The lump attached to the other cheek. The old man cried, saying, "Now I have two lumps!" and he went home.

The end.

DOWNLOAD LINK

Download Link for the MP3s:

http://japanesereaders.com/1030

Thank you for purchasing and reading this book! To contact the authors, please email them at help@thejapanshop.com. See also the wide selection of materials for learning Japanese at www.TheJapanShop.com and the free site for learning Japanese www.thejapanesepage.com.

CPSIA information can be obtained
at www.ICGtesting.com
Printed in the USA
LVHW081912200822
726390LV00002B/361